# XTREME ART

# DRAW MANGA MONSTERS!

## CHRISTOPHER HART

WATSON-GUPTILL PUBLICATIONS/NEW YORK

# INTRODUCTION

Manga monsters are everywhere! Originally from Japan, where they appear in comic books and TV shows, manga monsters have invaded our shores and have lots of fans. One of the great things about manga monsters is that they're so cute! Don't you wish you could have one as a pet? Well, you can have the next best thing: You can draw them. And with a little practice, you can even invent your own. In Japan, manga monsters are usually drawn as friends of human characters, but they can also be enemies. So be careful!

This book will help you draw all kinds of manga monsters. Each drawing is broken down into four simple steps. Start by tracing or drawing step 1. Then add the red lines in steps 2, 3, and 4. It's that easy!

The fun part about drawing manga monsters is that each one is unique. Some are fluffy, some are chubby, and some are even mean. A few of the manga monster drawings in this book have backgrounds, which you can either trace or draw if you like. Are you ready to make the world of manga monsters leap off the page? Grab a pencil and some paper and let's get started!

# Tips for Using This Book

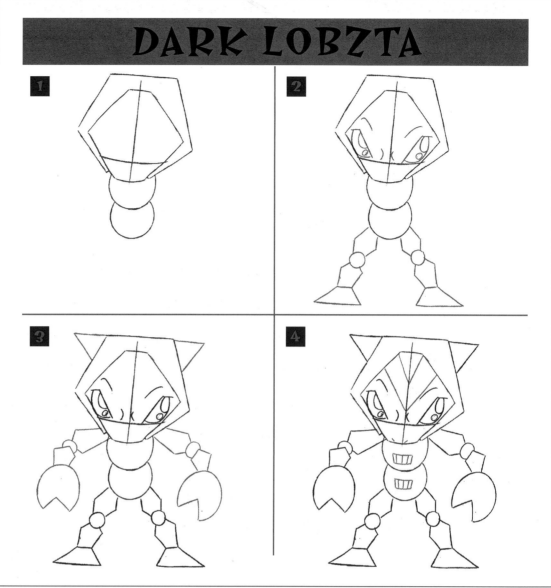

## DARK LOBZTA

1
2
3
4

Trace or draw what you see in step 1. Then add the new lines (shown in red) in steps 2, 3, and 4. Draw with a light, sketchy line. Don't worry about getting it perfect on the first try.

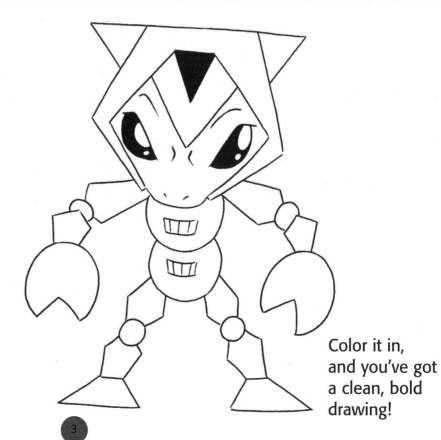

When you've finished the steps, erase the guidelines (the criss-crosses) and any other lines you don't want to keep. Go over the other lines to make them darker.

Color it in, and you've got a clean, bold drawing!

# THE BASICS

How do you make a monster? Surprisingly, it often begins with a chubby, simple little character. By adding bits and pieces as you go, you gradually build it into a unique creature. Only you can decide whether it will fight on the side of good...or evil!

1. START WITH A CHUBBY SHAPE.

2. ADD HORNS AND HAIR.

3. BIG WINGS MAKE IT MORE IMPRESSIVE.

4. NOW ADD FUN DETAILS, LIKE MARKINGS, A TUMMY CIRCLE, AND A TAIL!

Manga artists often use body shapes from real animals that they combine or change to create an original manga monster. Let's take a look at some popular sources of inspiration.

## Little Animals
This one has the body of a cat and the ears of a rabbit. The mane and long tail are additions that turn it into a manga monster.

## Worms, Crustaceans, and Insects
Worms, crustaceans, and insects are good beginnings for manga monsters. A worm body with crab-like hands does the trick for this character.

## Animals That Stand Like People
Giving an animal the posture of a human is a common way to make a manga monster. This one looks like a bull, but the tail has been changed to make it monster-ish.

## Exotic Animals and Lizards
Lizards and weird creatures like armadillos are great inspirations for manga monsters.

## Birds
Bird-type monsters are popular, especially those based on birds from the times of the dinosaurs, like the pterodactyl.

## Dinosaurs
Dinosaurs can be changed to make manga monsters with special powers.

A manga monster may look just like its animal inspiration, or nothing like it at all. As an artist, it's up to you to decide how far you want to change it. Take a look at these examples.

MANGA MONSTER BASED ON A TEDDY BEAR

MANGA MONSTER BASED ON A RABBIT

MANGA MONSTER BASED ON AN OCTOPUS

MANGA MONSTER BASED ON A FUR BALL!

It's important that the hands and feet look as though they belong to the same monster. A sea creature would have sea-creature hands and sea-creature feet, not sea-creature hands and hooves for feet. See how the hands and feet on this page go together?

# Hands                    # Feet

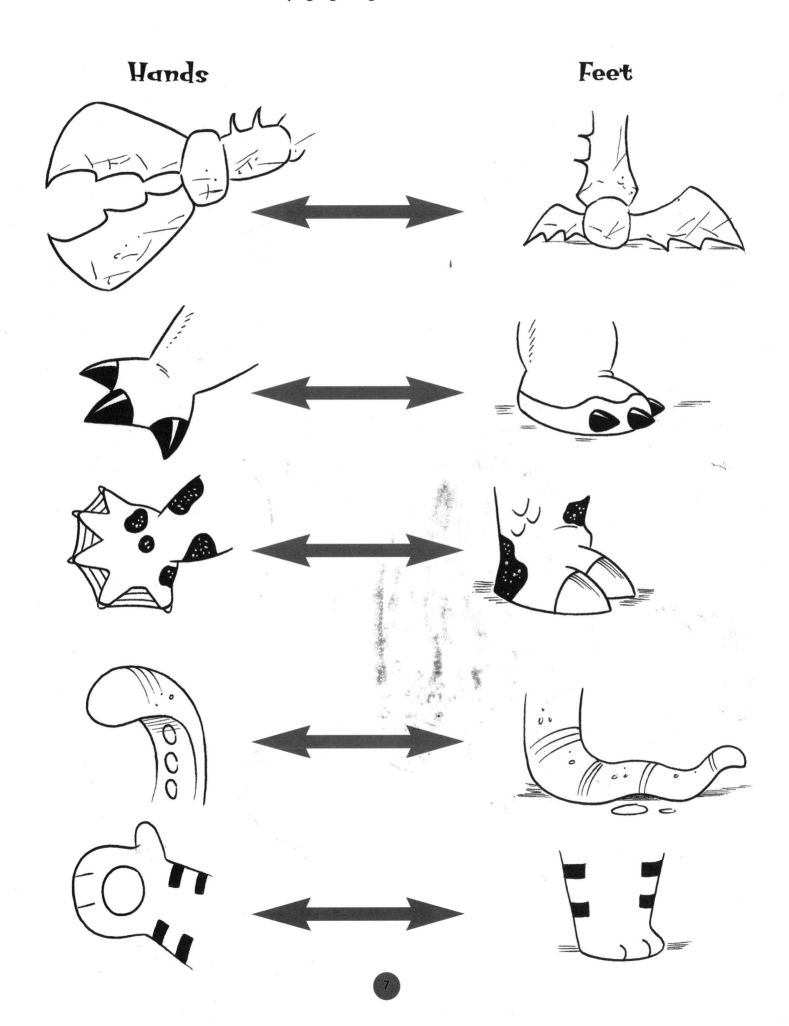

Eyes are a very important feature in manga characters, and they're especially important in manga monsters. Each monster should have its own, distinct type of eyes. Here are some popular types that you can draw.

BIG SHINE

SKINNY SHINE

EVIL EYES

DOUBLE SHINES

ALMOND-SHAPED EYES

BUTTON EYES

NOW TURN THE PAGE
AND START DRAWING
MANGA MONSTERS!

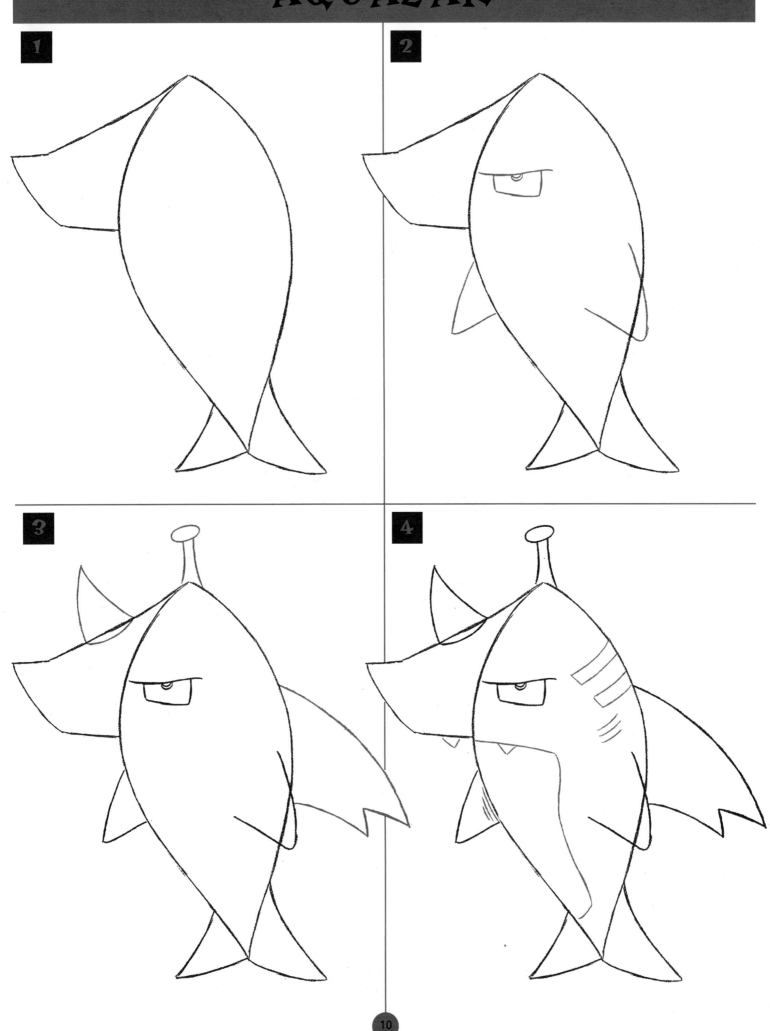

# BUBBLE BABY

**1**

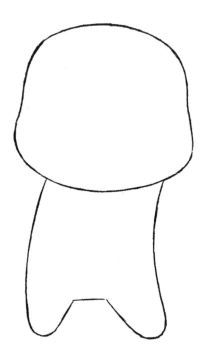

**2**

**3**

**4**

# PLUMPOON

**1**

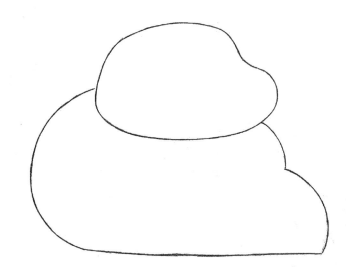

**2**

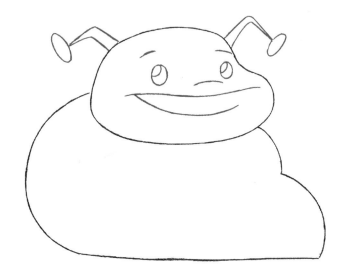

**3**

**4**

**1**

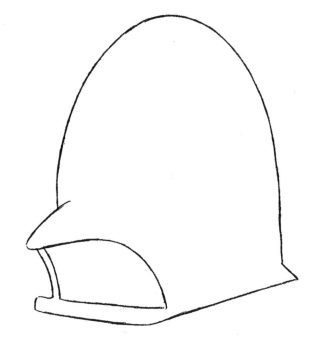

**2**

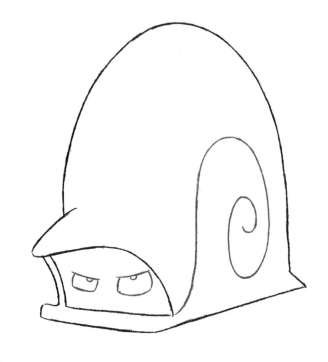

**3**

**4**

**1**

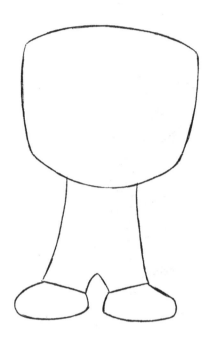

**2**

**3**

**4**

**1**

**2**

**3**

**4**

**1**

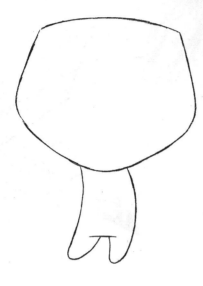

**2**

**3**

**4**

**1**

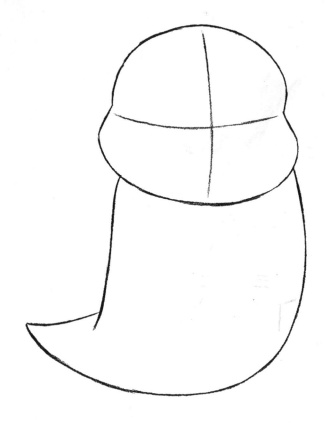

**2**

**3**

**4**

# FURTRON

1

2

3

4

# CHIMNEEK

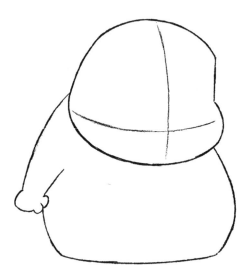

# COOBOO

1
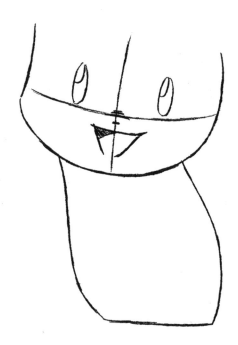

2

3

4

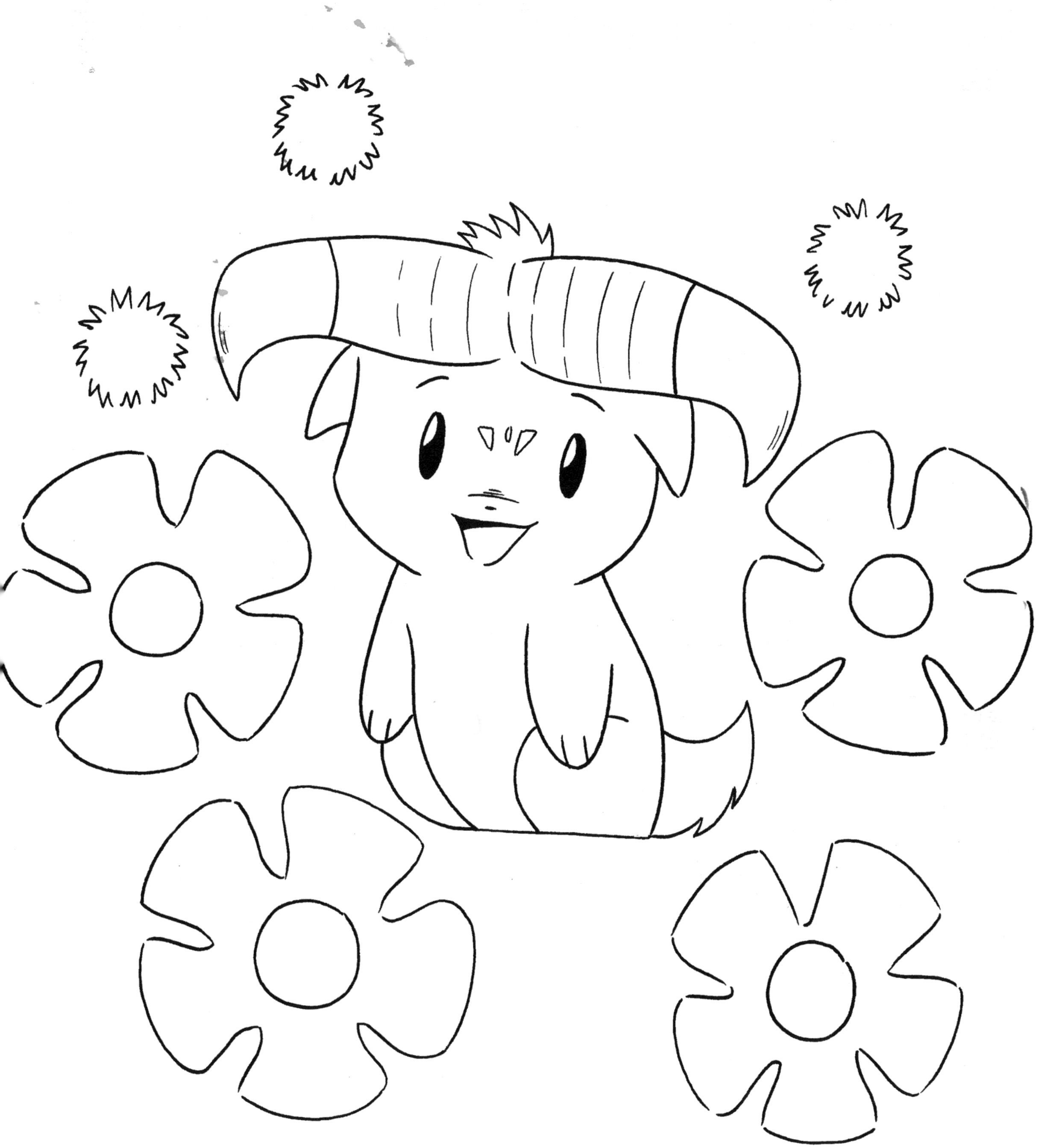

# VOLTOX

**1**

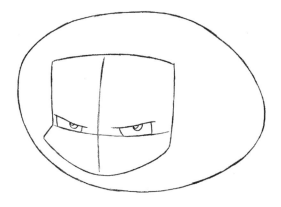

**2**

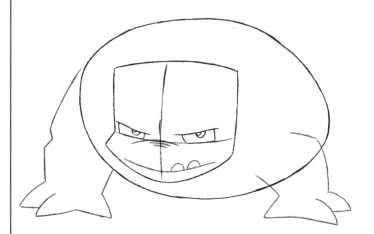

**3**

**4**

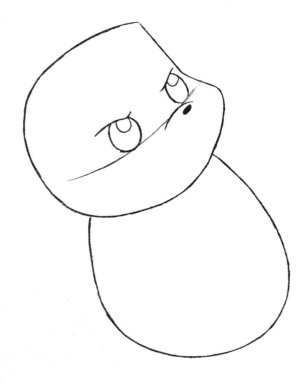

**1**

**2**

**3**

**4**

# MEGASPIKE

**1**

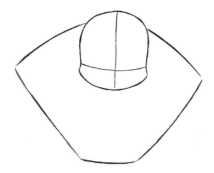

**2**

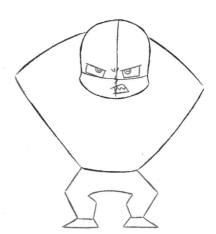

**3**

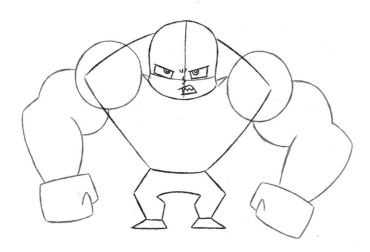

**4**

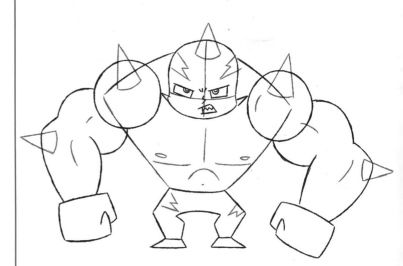

**1**

**2**

**3**

**4**

# ZIGZAGGER

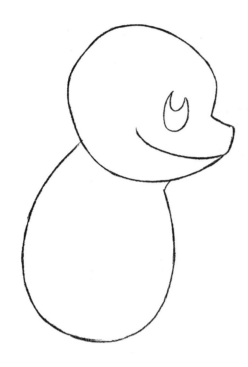

# ZYRK

**1**

**2**

**3**

**4**

**1**

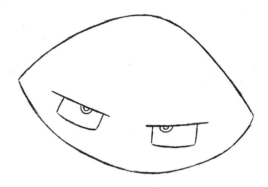

**2**

**3**

**4**

# DOLPHNEENA

**1**

**2**

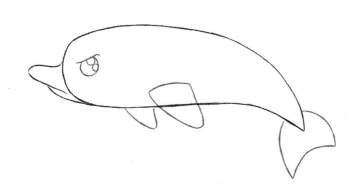

**3**

**4**

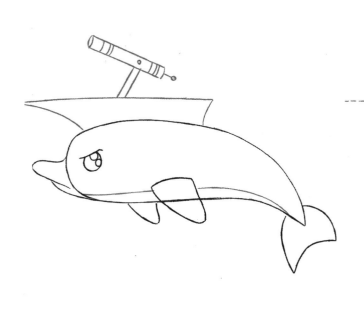

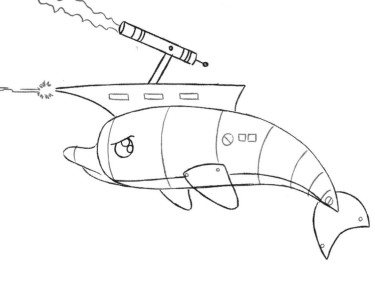

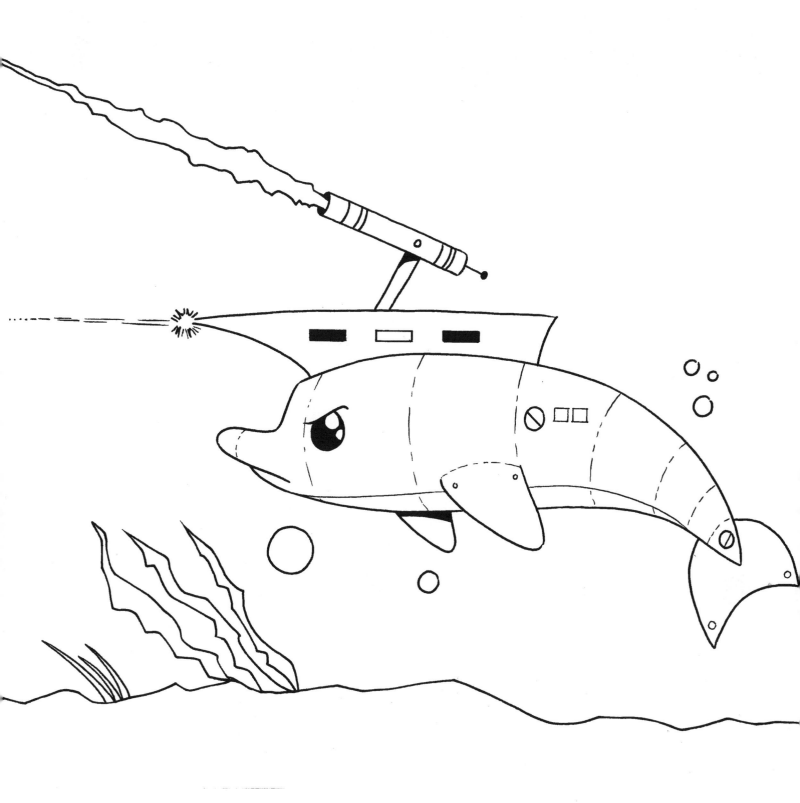

**1**

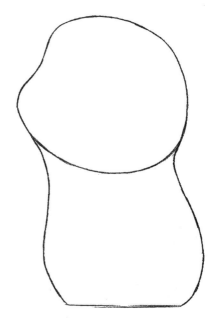

**2**

**3**

**4**

**1**

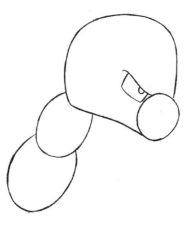

**2**

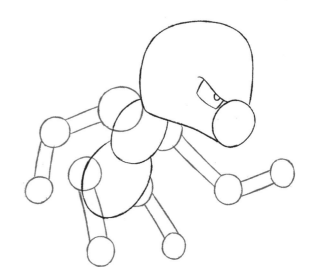

**3**

**4**

**1**

**2**

**3**

**4**

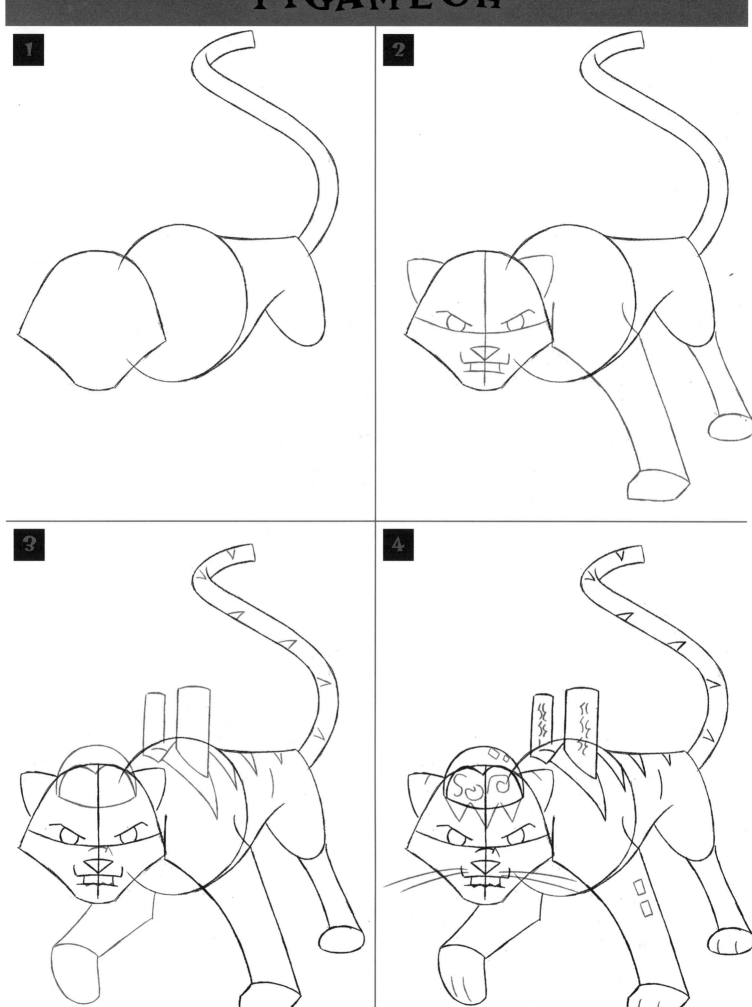

# CORAFLAME

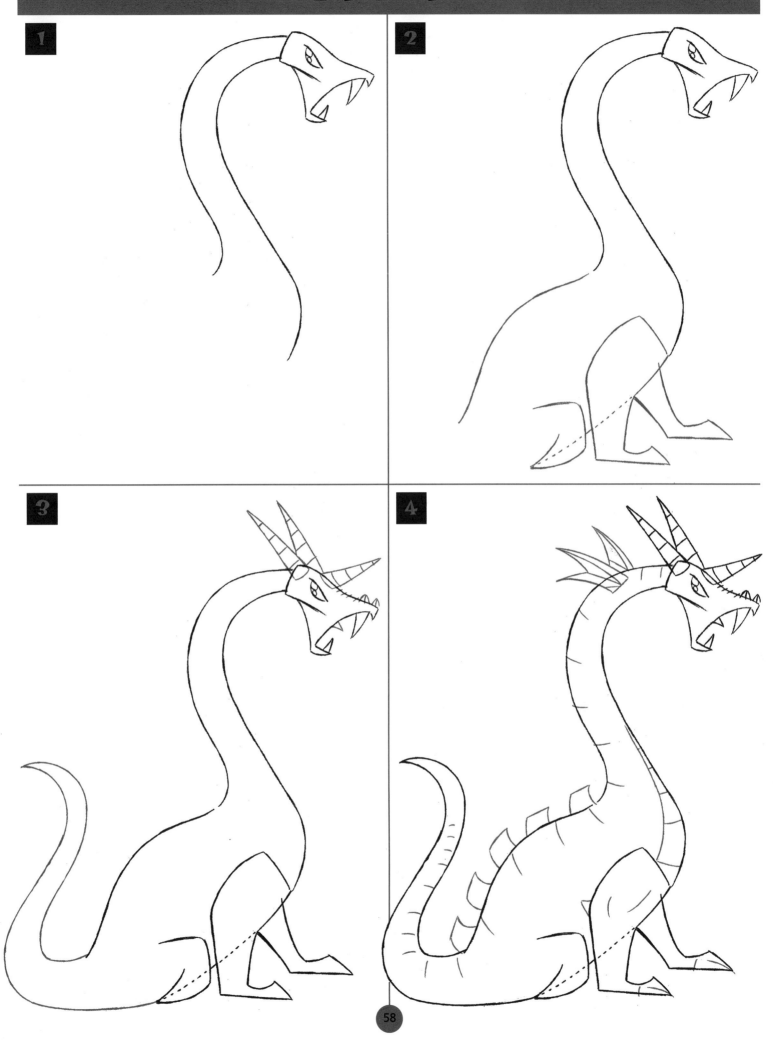

# PIPTAR 1 AND PIPTAR 2

**1**

**2**

**3**

**4**